LADIES' DAY

ARISTOPHANES

LADIES' DAY

AN ENGLISH VERSION
BY DUDLEY FITTS

HARCOURT, BRACE AND COMPANY

NEW YORK

for CORNELIA

Τὼ Θεσμοφόρω δ'
ἡμῖν ἀγαθήν
τούτων χάριν ἀνταποδοῖτον.

INTRODUCTORY NOTE

Thesmophoriazûsae was first produced in Athens at the Great Dionysia of 411 B.C. The unwieldy title is even more awkward in translation, for we should have to say something like 'The Women Keep the Thesmophorian Festival,' which is clear enough, but not particularly stimulating. It is one of the three plays—the others being *Lysistrata* and *The Women's Parliament*—in which Aristophanes handles the idea of women interfering in men's affairs, and this may be a reason why the comedy did not take first prize at the Dionysia. Another reason may be the fact that so much of the play is literary parody. There is action enough: some of the rough-&-tumble is as hearty as anything in the comic theatre; but it must be confessed that an extended burlesque of any poet, even a Euripides, lacks popular appeal. Nevertheless there is great vigour here, of a heady kind, and even this special kind of fun has overtones that reach us across the centuries.

When the infamous and vivid Publius Clodius disguised himself as a woman and intruded upon the rites of the Bona Dea in Julius Caesar's house, he was, consciously or not, reënacting the plot of our comedy. The Thesmophoria, the annual Feast of

Demeter and Persephonê, was sacred to women. What the rites were, the holy mysteries, we do not know; we can suppose that they were awful enough, and that the men-folk had their own ribald conjectures as to what went on; and we can be sure that the presence of a male was unthinkable, a kind of profanation. Clodius paid for his indiscretion, and Caesar's poor wife paid even more; but our hero Mnesilochos, who not only invades the forbidden precincts but has the temerity to speak up in open meeting, gets off with a few bruises, a great deal of humiliation, and a broad education in what might be called the Early Stanislavski Method. It is not given every old man to play, in one afternoon, the rôles of Helen of Troy and the princess Andrómeda *vis-à-vis* the Author himself; and we can believe that Mnesilochos is as glad as anyone in the house to hear the final words of the Chorus: 'It is late, and we have been playing long enough.' He is a scandalous old man, and Euripides is not much better; but they have beheld the Mysteries, made their point, and got off free.

The play is a friendly attack upon Euripides. (Another and minor poet, Agathôn, is less amiably handled in the Prologue, but it is Euripides who is the principal butt.) Why Euripides? First of all, because he was a shock: his innovations outraged authority and threatened the established conventions of the tragic stage, and his iconoclastic treatment of religious and social questions had already identified him with the new science, the new philosophy. Euripides, like Ibsen, was one of those germinal artists who both enchant men and make them think. Artists of this kind are never welcomed by the guardians of social order.

An aristocrat and conservative—and Aristophanes was both—will distrust them instinctively. Add the petty but exacerbating flames of literary intrigues, the interminable cliquish squabblings of writers and artists among themselves, and you have reason enough for an attack upon Euripides. The wonder is that it is so good-humoured; for while it is true that the dramatist takes a merciless drubbing at the hands of Aristophanes, it is also true that the very magnitude of the attack, the documentation itself, must be accounted a compliment of the most flattering kind. Such brilliant parody implies admiration, however qualified that admiration may be.

It also poses a problem for the translator. When Mnesilochos, ridiculous in his saffron gown, starts chanting the verses of the Ethiopian princess chained naked on the sea-shore rock, and Euripides, equally ridiculous in the stage device that lifts him above the scene, begins to intone the lines of Perseus, son of God—that is visual parody, and it can be managed. The verses themselves are a different matter. When a Euripidean original survives, as the *Helen* does, we can see what changes the parodist has made—generally they are not in the direction of verbal caricature—and estimate their effect upon an audience already familiar with the original. When the original has been lost, like the *Andrómeda,* we can only speculate. What we can not do, however, is to achieve the same effect in English by using the same means: quiet verbal parody no longer serves, and the only solution that I have been able to find is caricature and burlesque. The *disjecta membra* of Shakspere, the Border Ballads, popular tear-jerkers, and badly remembered passages from various devotional works, are far from being thoughtless or accidental: they are one way of suggesting the hundreds of quotations, misquotations, and overt and hidden allusions with which Aristophanes has salted this extraordinary poem.

It remains to be said that for my translation I have used the Budé text established by Victor Coulon, with aberrations whenever I have been attracted elsewhere by Rogers and the Oxford editors. The numbers at the head of each page give the lineation of the Greek text.

DF

CONTENTS

PERSONS REPRESENTED:

MNESILOCHOS	FIRST WOMAN (MIKA)
EURIPIDES	SECOND WOMAN (KRITYLLA)
SERVANT TO AGATHON	KLEISTHENES
AGATHON	A MAGISTRATE
A WOMAN HERALD	A POLICEMAN

CHORUS OF ATHENIAN WOMEN

The supernumeraries include MANIA a slave, FLEURETTE a dancing-girl, TEREDON a fluteplayer, and various servants and attendants.

The scene is Athens: before the house of Agathôn, in the Prologue, and thereafter in the Thesmophorion, the temple of Demeter and Persephonê.

PROLOGUE

PROLOGUE

[*Before the house of* AGATHON. *Enter the tragic poet* EURIPIDES *and his father-in-law* MNESILOCHOS. *Both are quite bald, patriarchally bearded, and richly dressed. They seem apprehensive, and* MNESILOCHOS *is obviously exhausted.*]

cf. shelley – Ode to West Wind

MNESILOCHOS:

'If winter comes,' they say . . . Yes, but this writer
has been riding herd on me ever since dawn,
and I'm a wreck.

         —For God's sake, Euripides,
before my guts give way entirely,
tell me where we're going.

EURIPIDES:

                Never seek to hear
what soon you will behold with your own eyes.

MNESILOCHOS:

How's that? Say it again. 'Never seek to hear'?

EURIPIDES:

What you're destined to see.

MNESILOCHOS:

             And never seek to see—

EURIPIDES:

What you're destined to hear.

MNESILOCHOS:

           I wish you would explain.
You seem to be trying to make sense. Do you mean
I do not need to hear what I do not see?

EURIPIDES:

    Right. The acoustic and the optic faculties
    are distinct by nature.

MNESILOCHOS:

                Not seeing and not hearing
    are different things?

EURIPIDES:

              That's exactly it.

MNESILOCHOS:

    How did that happen?

EURIPIDES:

                It goes back to the Creation.
    When Æther sifted out the first elements
    and brought the seeds of living things to light,
    he invented Vision, an eye round like the sun,
    and for Hearing he sunk a shaft right through the head.

MNESILOCHOS:

    And this is the shaft I neither see nor hear with?
    How charming is divine Philosophy!

EURIPIDES:

    Stick around me and you'll learn all sorts of things.

MNESILOCHOS:

    I don't doubt it for a minute. Maybe you'll teach me
    how to become suddenly lame: I'm sick
    of this endless trotting around.

EURIPIDES:

              Step over here
    and lend me your ears.

4

MNESILOCHOS:

You have them.

EURIPIDES:

Do you perceive

that little door?

MNESILOCHOS:

I do. At least, I think so.

EURIPIDES:

Hush!

MNESILOCHOS:

Hush that little door?

EURIPIDES:

And hear.

MNESILOCHOS:

Hear that little door hush?

EURIPIDES:

That little door

leads to the studio of Agathôn

the tragic poet.

MNESILOCHOS:

Which Agathôn would that be?
You mean the one that looks like a gypsy,
the big guy?

EURIPIDES:

No, the other one.

MNESILOCHOS:

I've never seen him. The one with all the whiskers?

5

EURIPIDES:

You've never seen him?

MNESILOCHOS:

Damned if I have—at least,
so far as I know.

EURIPIDES:

And yet you've laid him. But there,
I suppose it didn't make much of an impression.

[*The house door is opened from within:*

Let's step aside for a moment.
Here's one of his servants coming out with hot coals
and branches of myrtle: an offering, probably,
to the difficult Muse of Poësy.

[*Enter* SERVANT *from the house:*

SERVANT:

Let each mortal tongue keep silence.
Bound no more, O bounding Ocean.
Still thy breath, O silent Æther.
The ninefold sisterhood of Muses
roosts beneath my Master's roof.

MNESILOCHOS:

Crap!

EURIPIDES:

Be quiet.

6

MNESILOCHOS:

What's he talking about?

SERVANT:

Let the feathered generations
seek their nests; in the forest
stray no more, ye footed fauna.

MNESILOCHOS:

Crap and double crap!

SERVANT:

Sweet-singing

Agathôn this day is going—

MNESILOCHOS:

To get screwed?

SERVANT:

Whose voice assails me?

MNESILOCHOS:

Silent Æther's.

SERVANT:

—to construct the

keel of a poetic drama.
He will twist the arching word-ribs,
whirl them on the wheel, conglutinate them, inspissate with meaning,
tropify them, cerify them,
drill them and cylindrify them—

MNESILOCHOS:

Whorify them.

7

SERVANT:

What sad scoffer
dares invade the Master's precincts?

MNESILOCHOS:

A scoffer with a cylindrical drill for you
and that sweet singer of yours,
a scoffer ready to arch your precincts and
conglutinate your inspissation.

SERVANT:

Is that a fact?
You must have been a card, a century or two ago.

EURIPIDES:

Never mind him, my good man. Just step inside
and tell Agathôn we're calling.

SERVANT:

Why bother?
He'll be coming right out, anyway.
He's begun a new poem, and these November breezes
congeal his imagery. He needs some sun.

EURIPIDES:

And what do we do meanwhile?

SERVANT:

Why, you wait.   [*Exit*

EURIPIDES:

Ah, what hath God in store for me this day?

MNESILOCHOS:

Exactly! I wish to heaven you'd tell me

8

what this business is all about. What's

the matter with you? Why these groans? Must you

keep your secret from your own father-in-law?

EURIPIDES:

Carking calamity crawls on my horizon.

MNESILOCHOS:

Be specific.

EURIPIDES:

This day, this dreadful day,

Euripides is doomed to live or die.

MNESILOCHOS:

I don't see why.

There are no courts in session, and the Assembly's

adjourned for the holidays.

EURIPIDES:

That's why I am doomed.

For years and years

the women of Athens have been laying for me,

and today they are having a meeting

over there in the Shrine to bring the plot to a head.

MNESILOCHOS:

What's their grievance?

EURIPIDES:

They pretend that I libel them

in my tragedies.

MNESILOCHOS:

That's no pretence, by Poseidon!

9

But haven't you some trick to save your skin?

EURIPIDES:

Yes. I have thought of asking this poet Agathôn
to sneak into the Shrine somehow.

MNESILOCHOS:

I see. And then?

EURIPIDES:

I want him to assemble with the Assembly and
plead my cause, if he has to.

MNESILOCHOS:

In disguise?

EURIPIDES:

In disguise, of course.

MNESILOCHOS:

As a woman?

EURIPIDES:

Naturally.

MNESILOCHOS:

I find that a charming idea.
Really, Euripides,
when it comes to subtlety, you take the cake!

EURIPIDES:

Hush!

MNESILOCHOS:

Now what?

EURIPIDES:

Here comes Agathôn.

10

MNESILOCHOS:

Where, where?

EURIPIDES:

There on the revolving porch.

MNESILOCHOS:

God, I'm going blind! All I can see
is that whore Kyrenê.

EURIPIDES:

For goodness' sake, be quiet!
He's going to sing.

MNESILOCHOS:

Runs and roulades, do you think,
or something in the more majestic line?

[*The revolving stage has brought out* AGATHON *lying
on a couch, holding a lyre. In this position he recites
the strophes of the following Litany; but for each
responsory* [℟] *he rises, turns towards where he has
been reclining, and performs as his own Chorus.*

AGATHON:

I summon a glory of torches whirled
In a maenad rout for the Spirits of Earth.
Dance freedom, maidens, dance happiness!
   ℟ *For whom shall we dance? For whom shall we dance?*
Lord Phoibos first, the golden Archer,
Builder of fair Simoïs' ramparts.

11

℞ *Apollo, Victor in art! Apollo,*
    Laurelled with eternal music!
Artemis also, Huntress immaculate,
Wanderer of the mountain woodlands.
    ℞ *O Lêto's Daughter, thou pure flame,*
       Artemis, Maid inviolate!
Strike sweetness from the Asian lyre:
Circle the goddess, O Phrygian Graces!
    ℞ *Holy harp, O Spring of song,*
       Male art joined with woman's voice!
       Her eyes are intolerable fire
       As we rejoice
       Singing the Artemis dance, the Apollo dance.

        [AGATHON *resumes his couch. Attendants cluster*
        about him with incense, fans, bottles.

MNESILOCHOS:

  By the gods and goddesses of copulation,
  that was a delightful melody!
  All womanish along the tongue and kissy, I swear,
  it went straight to my arse.

                        —Young man,
  whoever you are, permit me to address you
  in the style of Aischylos:
      'What woman, or what man, or both
      Combinèd, with cosmetic art
      Bewrays the stigma of his youth

                    12

    I' th' costume of a virile tart?'
I understand the lyre, of course; but what
are you doing with a hair-net? A bottle
of gymnasium oil, yes; but why the girdle?
Why a hand-mirror and a sword at the same time?
What are you, you recumbent paradox? A man?
Show me; or, if that makes you blush,
where are your Spartan boots, your cavalry cloak?
Or are you a woman? If so, where are your breasts?
No answer. Bashful. If I want to find out,
I suppose I'll have to read your *Collected Poems*.

AGATHON:

Greybeard, greybeard, your malicious envy
bombards my ears, but I heed it not at all.
However, if you must know,
I wear this particular costume by design.
A dramatist embarked upon his art
should prepare for the voyage; and since my best plays
are female, my manner suggests the Heroine.
Do you follow me?

MNESILOCHOS:

                More or less. I take it
You're barearse when you go to work on a *Phaidra*.

AGATHON:

Again, a male rôle calls for male properties.
Thus art makes up for natural defect.

13

MNESILOCHOS:

Remember me when you write a satyr play:
I've a fundamental art that will enchant you.

AGATHON:

Furthermore, who wants a hairy poet?
Bah, these rugged artists!

                        No, let me have
Ibykos—there's a writer for you!—or Anakreôn
or Alkaios, all of them simply a-swim with music.
Those boys liked pretty hats and pretty manners,
and that's the reason their songs are pretty, too.
Or take Phrynichos—you've heard of him, surely:
he was a fancy poet with a fancy taste,
and his fancy poems go fancying down the ages.
It's a law of nature:
Art is the perfect mirror of character.

MNESILOCHOS:

Is that why Philoklês writes horrible trash,
and Xenoklês writes filth, and that man Theognis,
cold as a haddock, writes frozen monodies?

AGATHON:

Obviously. And that, my dear sir, is why
I spend such loving care upon my person.

MNESILOCHOS:

Balls for your loving care!

EURIPIDES:

                    Oh let him alone.

I was like that myself when I began writing.

MNESILOCHOS:

Really? I suppose that explains a great deal.

EURIPIDES:

Let's change the subject.

                              —My dear Agathôn,
allow me to tell you why I'm here.

AGATHON:

                                        Tell me.

EURIPIDES:

Brevity, someone has said, is the soul of wit.
I will be brief.

                              —Agathôn, you perceive here
a suppliant with an unheard-of problem.

AGATHON:

What problem?

EURIPIDES:

                              Women, as usual.
They're meeting in the Thesmophorion today,
and the single dreadful purpose of that meeting
is to ruin Euripides. They say I've insulted them.

AGATHON:

What could I do?

EURIPIDES:

                              You could do anything;
but what I have in mind is
that you get yourself into the meeting (it's easy enough

for you to pass as a woman) and make a speech
for me at the proper time. That would save my life.
Will you do it? After all,
I could hardly find a more appropriate spokesman.

AGATHON:

Why not go and make the speech yourself?

EURIPIDES:

I'll tell you. First of all, they know me;
secondly—well, I'm not so young as I was,
silver threads among the gold, you know, and this beard
is fairly long. But you're handsome and smoothcheeked
with a ladylike voice and delicate way. You'd do.

AGATHON:

Euripides.

EURIPIDES:

Yes?

AGATHON:

Do you remember once writing:
'You love the sun; do you think your father does not?'

EURIPIDES:

I wrote it.

AGATHON:

And now you propose to shove off your problems
onto me. Do I look crazy? No, no, I tell you,
calamity must be met with guts, not guile.
You've got to bear your own bad luck.

16

MNESILOCHOS:

>You'll bare
that arse of yours, and that's no figure of speech!

EURIPIDES:

What are you afraid of?

AGATHON:

>I'd be even worse than you.

EURIPIDES:

How so?

AGATHON:

>The women would think
that I had come with Lesbian intentions.

MNESILOCHOS:

Your intentions are all *a posteriori*, friend.
Just the same, it's a reasonable excuse.

EURIPIDES:

>For the last time:
Will you do it?

AGATHON:

>What do *you* think?

EURIPIDES:

>Then farewell,
a long farewell to all Euripides' greatness!

MNESILOCHOS:

O friend! O relative! Be not dismayed.

EURIPIDES:

Why not?

17

MNESILOCHOS:

Forget about this Agathôn.

Here I am. Take me. Do what you like.

EURIPIDES:

You mean it?

Off with that cloak, then!

MNESILOCHOS:

Off it goes. What next?

EURIPIDES:

Well, those whiskers of yours; and lower down.

MNESILOCHOS:

If you say so. Might as well go the whole hog.

EURIPIDES:

Agathôn, you're always shaving: will you lend us
a razor?

AGATHON:

You'll find one over there in the box.

EURIPIDES:

Kind of you.

—Now, father-in-law, sit down here
and stick out your cheek.

MNESILOCHOS:

Ouch!

EURIPIDES:

What's the matter?

Have I got to gag you?

18

MNESILOCHOS:

Ouch! Suffering God!

EURIPIDES:

Come back here! Where are you off to?

MNESILOCHOS:

A sanctuary.

By God, I'm not going to stay here and get carved.

EURIPIDES:

They'll laugh at you with half your face shaved clean.

MNESILOCHOS:

Let them laugh.

EURIPIDES:

Oh come now, for heaven's sake,

think of me for a change.

MNESILOCHOS:

I have no character.

All right. Go ahead.

EURIPIDES:

Sit down.

—Stop fidgeting.

Puff your other cheek out.

MNESILOCHOS:

Woof.

EURIPIDES:

What do you mean, 'woof'?

—There! That's a handsome job, if I *do* say so!

MNESILOCHOS:

Who said a soldier's bearded like the pard?

EURIPIDES:

Never mind that. *I* think you're dazzling.

Would you like to look at yourself?

MNESILOCHOS:

Hand me that glass.

—My God, I'm looking at Kleisthenês!

EURIPIDES:

Stand up.

Bend over. Here goes the rest of the foliage.

MNESILOCHOS:

Stop! Must I be singed like a pig on a platter?

EURIPIDES:

Bring a torch, boy, or a lamp to put under him.

—Stoop over. There. Keep your tail out of the flame.

MNESILOCHOS:

I certainly will.

—Water! Water!

Ring the alarm! There's fire down below!

EURIPIDES:

Keep cool.

MNESILOCHOS:

When my poop's a howling holocaust?

EURIPIDES:

Don't worry. The worst is over.

20

MNESILOCHOS:

I believe you.

The crater's full of soot.

EURIPIDES:

We'll sponge it out.

MNESILOCHOS:

God pity the man who sponges *that* abyss.

EURIPIDES:

Agathôn, you won't lend yourself, but you might
let us have a dress and a brassière, at least,
for his costume. Don't tell us you can't.

AGATHON:

Take what you need.

EURIPIDES:

Let's see. Which gown?

AGATHON:

Why not that saffron one?

It's simply darling.

MNESILOCHOS:

It smells darling, all right.

Now where's that breast gadget?

EURIPIDES:

Here you are.

MNESILOCHOS:

Is my slip showing?

EURIPIDES:

You're all right. Now

21

something ribbony for your head.

AGATHON:

This precious toque.

EURIPIDES:

Toqué!

MNESILOCHOS:

Does it suit me?

EURIPIDES:

It's a dream.

Now a fur stole.

AGATHON:

There's one on the divan.

EURIPIDES:

And slippers?

AGATHON:

Take the ones I'm wearing.

MNESILOCHOS:

They'll fit me?

I know you like things loose.

AGATHON:

They'll fit to a T.
—And now, if you have everything you want,
I think I'll have myself wheeled back inside.

> [*The inner stage revolves, carrying off* AGATHON *and
> his ménage.*

EURIPIDES:

Well, my dear hermaphrodite,

I hope you'll remember to speak like a woman in there.

MNESILOCHOS:

Goodneth me, I'll do my betht.

EURIPIDES:

I'm sure of it.

Well, let's be going.

MNESILOCHOS:

Not yet, by Apollo!

Not until you swear—

EURIPIDES:

Swear what?

MNESILOCHOS:

That if the worst

happens, as it probably will, you'll do *your* best

to rescue *me*.

EURIPIDES:

I swear it by the Æther,

the house of Zeus on high.

MNESILOCHOS:

You might as well

swear by that sty of Hippokratês's.

EURIPIDES:

I swear by all the heavenly gods at once.

MNESILOCHOS:

Remember,

23

it is your heart, and not your tongue, that swears.
I insist on the distinction.

EURIPIDES:

We must hurry.
They've raised the signal on Deméter's shrine.
I'm off. Good bye, good luck!

[*Exeunt separately.*

24

PÁRODOS

[The Thesmophorion, or Temple of Demeter and Persephonê. Women of all ages are assembling about a central altar behind which, on a platform, is the speakers' rostrum. MNESILOCHOS *enters mincingly, addressing an imaginary maidservant. At the end of his speech he attempts to lose himself in the group nearest the rostrum.*

MNESILOCHOS:

Thratta, Thratta, keep close to me, Thratta,
over this way, Thratta. Mercy, all that lamp-smoke!
And the crowds! I declare,
I never saw anything like it, Thratta.

                  —But
I ought to be saying my prayers:

                      Loveliest Goddesses,
hear me, be gracious to me now, and when I get home.

—Look in the basket, Thratta:
I want the little holy cake to offer
to the Goddesses.

            —O Deméter, august Lady,
and thou, Persephonê: grant that I
may bring my gifts to you time and time again,
or at least that no one recognize me this time.
Grant that little Pussy, my dear dear daughter,
may find a rich young man to marry her,
yes, and a silly young man, too; and grant

27

my dear son Jock a modicum of horse sense.
Amen.

       —Goodness me, where's the best place to sit?
—You run along home, Thratta. It isn't right
for servants to hear the things we ladies say.

          [*A* WOMAN HERALD *mounts the rostrum:*

WOMAN HERALD:
Silentium! Silentium!

Let us pray:

To Deméter and Persephoneia Givers of Law; to Ploutos and
    to Kalligeneia; to Mother Earth Nourisher of Youth; to
    Hermês; to the Graces also: That the deliberations and
    enactments of this Assembly be crowned with success for
    Athens and for the Women of Athens; and that what
    woman soever this day thinks clearest and speaks best may
    triumph in the cause for the which she pleads.
Iê Paián! Iê Paián! Iê Paián!

Lift up your hearts.

CHORAGOS:
Let us pray to the blest Gods.

       [*The following passage is Versicle (solo voice) with
       choral Responsory:*

CHORUS:
  ℣ Zeus, thou Name of Awe, hear us.

℟ Zeus, thou Name of Awe, hear us.

℣ Regent of holy Dêlos, god golden-lyred:

℟ Apollo, hear us.

℣ O mighty Maiden whose flashing eyes and lance of gold
      blaze in high Athens:

℟ Athêna, hear us.

℣ O Huntress, golden Lêto's Child,
      O thou of many names:

℟ Artemis, hear us.

℣ Thou Lord of the fish-thronged ways of Ocean:

℟ Poseidon, hear us.

℣ O all ye Water Nymphs, Daughters of Nêreus: and ye,
      Oreadês, Nymphs of the mountain reaches:

℟ Hear us, be near us.

℣ May the Golden Lyre
      inspire our song.

℟ May our noble Assembly
      conclude in joy.

CHORAGOS:

In the name of the Gods and Goddesses of Olympos:

in the name of the Pythian Goddesses and Gods:

in the name of the Gods and Goddesses Delian: and in the
  name

of all other Divinities:

Hear our Commination:

29

CHORUS:

℣   Cursèd be he who shall conspire
      against the Council of Women:

℟   Cursèd be he.

℣   Cursèd be he who shall consort with the Persians
      or with Euripides:

℟   Cursèd be he.

℣   Cursèd be he who shall work to restore the Tyranny,
      or shall think to make himself Tyrant:

℟   Cursèd be he.

℣   Cursèd be he who shall betray
      the supposititiousness of any woman's child:

℟   Cursèd be he.

℣   Cursèd be any confidential handmaid
      who shall betray her mistress to her master:

℟   Cursèd be she.

℣   Cursèd be any slave who shall misrepresent
      a message sent to a lover:

℟   Cursèd be she.

℣   Cursèd be any exasperated old woman
      who shall attempt to buy a young man's love:

℟   Cursèd be she.

℣   Cursèd be any lover
      who shall seduce with promises, and break them:

℟   Cursèd be he.

℣   Cursèd be any young woman
      who shall take a lover's treat, and deny her body:

30

℞   Cursèd be she.

℣   Cursèd be any bartender or barmaid
    who shall falsify measures of wine, be they pints or
    quarts.

℞   Cursèd be he or she.

℣   Let all such wretches wither at the root:

℞   Yea, let their house and household perish for ever.

℣   As for us, may the high Gods bless us
    and keep us in comfort all the days of our life.

℞   Seeing that all they stand accurst
          Who stood in need of cursing,
      Heav'n grant that we avoid the worst
          Of what we've been rehearsing.

      The women's laws enacted here
          Shall not by us be broken;
      We'll whisper in no hairy ear
          What, woman-like, we've spoken.

      We'll not connive against the peace
          For all the Great King's treasure;
      The dramas of Euripides
          Shall stir in us no pleasure.

      As women, we have known abuse;
          As women, we'll persever.
      To women grant thy strength, O Zeus,
          And smile on our endeavour.

31

AGON:α

WOMAN HERALD:

The meeting will please come to order
in accordance with the following Resolution:

'MOVED AND VOTED BY THE JUNTA OF WOMEN:
'To call an Assembly for the morning
'of the Middle Day of Thesmophoria,
'when women have least to do,
'to consider the case of Euripides
'and what action should be taken in it:
'it being the sense of this meeting
'that the activities of said Euripides
'render him liable to general censure.

> TIMOKLEIA, *Presiding Officer*
> SOSTRATE, *for the Motion*
> LYSILLA, *Secretary*'

Does any lady desire the floor?

FIRST WOMAN:

> I do.

WOMAN HERALD:

Assume the garland before you begin to speak.

> [FIRST WOMAN, *garlanded, mounts the rostrum:*

CHORAGOS:

Silence! No talking, please. Lend her your attention.
She clears her throat like one who has much to say.

35

FIRST WOMAN:

Ladies:

I call the Two Goddesses to witness
that it is not personal vanity that obliges me
to address you today. No; I have long
viewed with alarm the reprehensible conduct
of the vegetable dealer's son Euripides.
The vicious
contumely he has indulged in, dragging us
through the cloacine seepage of his mind!
Evil? Can you think of any evil
that he has left unsaid? Give him some actors,
a Chorus, an audience, and there he goes
proving that women are good-for-nothings, incarnate
wine-jugs, walking sinks of lust, deceivers,
babblers, fly-by-nights, knives in the flesh
of honest men. And what is the result?
You know perfectly well. When those husbands of ours
come home from one of his plays,
first they look at us queerly, and then,
why, they simply tear the house apart
hunting for lovers hidden in some closet.
It's no use,
we can't do things we've been doing all our lives
but they get suspicious, thanks to Euripides
and his Advice to Husbands.

Suppose a woman

36

buys a flower for her hair: that means she's in love.
Or she drops a pot or two on the way to the kitchen:
immediately her husband finds significance
in the broken crockery, and he quotes Euripides:
The trembling hand betrays th' adult'rous guest.
Or say a girl gets sick,
here comes big brother with his Euripides:
This morning greenness augureth no maid.
Bad enough;
but these men are into everything! Why, if a woman
can't have a baby and wants to buy one—you know—,
she hasn't a chance in the world, because there's her husband
camping out in front of the house. And that isn't all.
Think of the rich old men that used to marry
young girls. Do they do it any more? No. Why?
Because of Euripides and his wretched nonsense:
What's wedlock but enslavement to the old?
Do you see? And what's worse still,
our bedroom doors must now have special locks
and special keys, to keep us safe! And our houses
must be full of great growling wolfhounds from Molossos—
to keep us safe, and scare our lovers to death!
It's come to the point that we're no longer mistresses
in our own homes; we don't even control
our flour, our wine, any of our provisions.
These ridiculous men
have taken to using the horridest little keys

from Sparta, things with three teeth, hopeless
to try to cope with. The silliest penny ring
was good enough once to fake a seal on the door;
but now this family curse, this Euripides,
has taught our men to use fussy private signets
that you simply can't copy—and, what's worse,
they carry them around on chains hitched under their ears.

Ladies, I could say much more; and, with your permission,
I shall extend my remarks in the official Minutes.
Meanwhile, in view of the abuses that I have mentioned,
I move that Euripides be taken care of
in some permanent and unpleasant way: poison,
perhaps, or a more subtle medium.

                        Ladies, I move
the abolition of Euripides!

CHORUS:

            Oh woman's tongue! Persuasion,   [STROPHE
               Conviction, honest sense!
            What masculine evasion
               Can twist her evidence?
            She disentangles fact from lie
            And puts to blush male sophistry.

            Now Justice laughs victorious
               At grunting Error's frown.
            What man, however glorious,

Can talk a woman down?
Xenoklês himself would seem
An elocutionist's dry dream.

[*The* SECOND WOMAN *has taken her place at the ros-trum:*

SECOND WOMAN:

Ladies, unused as I am to public speaking,
I do want to put my little oar in. Everything
the last lady said was absolutely correct,
but I have a personal complaint.

—My man
got himself killed on Kypros, and that left me
with five little mouths to feed. Well, I managed
to make out, more or less, in the holiday wreath line
over in the myrtle market, you know, until
this person U. Ripides came along. He's in
the writing line himself, they tell me; and what
does he do but sell the carriage trade the idea
that there aren't any gods!

No gods! I ask you!
You can guess what happened to the wreath business then:
cut in half, it was.

Well, what I say,
this highbrow writer's dangerous, a wild man—
no wonder:
he was brought up on wild vegetables—and I say

39

he ought to be stopped.

                  Well, that's it.

That's all I have time for. We got an order

for twenty wreaths this morning, festival type,

and back to the old grind for yours truly. 'Bye now!

CHORUS:

> Her complex eloquence   [MESODE
> Sways the sense
> Even more
> Than the rhetoric before.
> No fuss,
> No animus,
> Pure passion, that's all.
> Euripides, here's check
> mate: on your neck
> Let the great axe fall.

[MNESILOCHOS *timidly mounts the rostrum:*

MNESILOCHOS:

Ladies, permit me to begin by saying

that I thoroughly sympathise with your grievance

against the so-called poet Euripides.

The mother's heart o' me burns—burns, I say—

with hatred for that reprobate. Damned if it doesn't.

However,

what I want to say is—just among us women,

no one listening in—, we've got to be awfully sure

40

we know what we're doing.

And, well, *are* we?

I mean, we let ourselves get all worked up
over this cad because he's told two or three home truths
about us, but when you come to think of it,
he hasn't said a word about the hundreds
and hundreds of things that we get away with
every day of our lives.

—Take me, for instance.
I won't speak for the rest of you, but I know
there's a lot of funny business on my conscience.
For example: It's
three days after the wedding, with my husband
snoring beside me. Well, I had a lover—
a sweet boy he was, too: made me a woman
on my seventh birthday—
and this night I'm talking about, he gets overcome
with emotion, and the first thing I know
I hear him scratching at the front door. Well,
I slip out of bed, just as easy as easy,
and all of a sudden up pops my husband's head.
'Where *you* going?' he says. 'Where?' says I,
all innocence, 'Why, *you* know where.
'I got a cramp. Something I ate.' 'Go ahead,' he says,
and damned if he doesn't get up too and start
boiling up a juniper-and-anise recipe
for that cramp!

41

Well, I get down to the door,
pour some water on the hinge to kill the squeaking,
and sure enough, there's the boy friend out in the street.
Well, I grab hold of the doorway shrine with one hand
and the laurel bush with the other, and bend over.
And that's the story.

But Euripides never told it.
As a matter of fact,
he's never mentioned the times we put ourselves out
to be nice to slaves and muledrivers when we can't find
anything better. He's never explained
how we chew garlic after a really hard night
so that when our husbands come home from guard duty
they won't smell what we've been up to.

—Isn't that your
experience, madam?

—And what if he does libel Phaidra?
What's Phaidra to us? At least he didn't tell
on the woman who stretched her cloak out at arm's length
to let her husband see how pretty it was,
while her lover was crawling out the window behind it!
No, or that other woman
pretending to have her pains for ten whole days
until she could buy a baby to fob off on her husband,
and all the time the poor man
running around town trying to find some medicines
to bring it on, till finally the midwife

42

smuggles a brat in—in a pot, with a gob of wax
down its gullet, to muffle the yells; and then,
when she gives the sign,
the wife moans: 'Darling, no men allowed! But this time
'I think I can promise you a son and heir.'
Exit husband. And then the old hag hauls the wax
out, pinches the papoose—and what a howl!
Reënter husband. The old fraud grins like a cat
and puts the evidence in the poor fish's arms:
'A lion!' she says, 'a regular little lion!
'The spitting image of you, sir, right down
'to his little acorn!'

          —No. We have our faults, Ladies,
I swear to Artemis we have. Should we really blame
Euripides, when we're so naughty ourselves?

CHORUS:

    Can I believe my twó eárs?   [ANTISTROPHE
      Who let this woman in?
    What are we going to do, dears?
      How can we ever win
    If this untutored female's spite
    Brings all our little sins to light?

    The current generation
      Has lost all sense of shame.
    Unhappy is the nation
      When women women blame!

Each stone (the proverb says) *conceals*
A friend—who'll smile, and sting your heels.

CHORAGOS:

Both ways from the girdle do the fiends inherit.
Your woman is a catastrophic spirit.

FIRST WOMAN:

Are you out of your mind? So help me Aglauros,
you've been hypnotized, or something else awful
has happened to you. This silly woman,
are we going to let her walk away with the meeting?

[*to the audience:*

Is there a gentleman in the house
who will help us?
                    —I see there is none; we'll have
to help ourselves. Come, tell the servants
to collect a pan of hot coals: a little singeing
in the proper place will make this person remember
her duty to speak well of other women.

MNESILOCHOS:

Oh not in the proper place, Sisters, not
in the proper place! Do I deserve
depilation? Never! What if I did say
some neutral things about Euripides?
This is a closed session, we have
freedom of speech, I only said what I thought.

44

FIRST WOMAN:

Freedom of speech? To defend Euripides?
You are the only one here
shameless enough to stand up for this man
whose one delight is the slander of womanhood.
Oh, he's a real artist when it comes
to painting your Phaidras and your Melanippês,
but he'll never never have a kindly word
for a solid citizen like Penelopê.

MNESILOCHOS:

There's a good reason for that. You won't find
a single Penelopê alive today,
only Phaidras and Phaidras and daughters of Phaidra.

FIRST WOMAN:

Do you hear her, Ladies? The slut
sums us all up and damns us with one word.

MNESILOCHOS:

Mercy, I haven't told
the millionth part of what we're capable of
Do you want me to go on?

FIRST WOMAN:

You couldn't.
You've poured out all the filth you know.

MNESILOCHOS:

Not

the millionth part of it! Shall I tell
how we use our strigils to siphon off the grain—

FIRST WOMAN:

Damn your grain!

MNESILOCHOS:

Or how we give our go-betweens
the food and drink saved up for festival days,
and blame it on the cat?

FIRST WOMAN:

Atheistical communism!

MNESILOCHOS:

Shall I tell about the woman
who chopped her husband up with a hatchet? No.
Or the one who drove her husband crazy with drugs?
No. Or the other one, that Acharnian—

FIRST WOMAN:

Stop it!

MNESILOCHOS:

—who hid her father's body under the bathtub?

FIRST WOMAN:

Shut up!

MNESILOCHOS:

Shall I tell them how you yourself
switched new-born babies with one of your own slaves
in order to get a boy instead of a girl?

FIRST WOMAN:

No, by the Goddesses, you needn't. But I'll
tell you what I have in mind: I'm going
to snatch you baldheaded!

46

MNESILOCHOS:

You and who else?

FIRST WOMAN:

Come on, you!   [*she strips for action:*

MNESILOCHOS:

Come on, you!

FIRST WOMAN:

Hold my dress, Philistê.

MNESILOCHOS:

Touch but a hair of this grey head, by Artemis,
and I'll—

FIRST WOMAN:

You'll what?

MNESILOCHOS:

I'll pound the breakfast out of you!

CHORAGOS:

Ladies, ladies, this debate is unpleasant.
Besides, there's a woman coming. What a haste
looks through her eyes! Let us compose ourselves
and hear what she has to say.

[*Enter* KLEISTHENES, *elegant in dress, affected and
effeminate in speech:*

KLEISTHENES:

Darlingest ladies, what *is* going on?
I've been hearing the awfullest things
down in the Agora, something about a perfectly

47

horrid practical joke.

You know—

I don't have to tell *you*—how close I feel
to you. I've been mad about women all my life,
and your little problems are mine. So I am here
this bright morning to warn you to look out
for a too too *nasty* surprise.

CHORAGOS:

What surprise, dear boy?
I hope you don't mind my calling you 'dear boy':
those sweet smooth cheeks . . .

KLEISTHENES:

What they're *saying* is
that Euripides has sneaked a vile old man,
some relative of his, into your Assembly.

CHORAGOS:

Why would he do that?

KLEISTHENES:

To spy on you.
It seems he's worried about your intentions.

CHORAGOS:

A man unnoticed among all these women? Absurd.

KLEISTHENES:

Darling, he's *shaved* and *plucked*! Also dis*guised*!

MNESILOCHOS:

I never heard such a silly story. Really!

No man would ever let himself be plucked.
I don't believe a word of it.

KLEISTHENES:

Do you think I'd invent
a thing like that? My information comes
from usually reliable sources.

CHORAGOS:

This is dreadful!
Quick, everyone, look around for this man,
sniff him out wherever he is, the old rogue
spying on us!

And you, Kleisthenês,
if you want to increase our obligation to you,
help us to find him.

KLEISTHENES (*to* FIRST WOMAN):

You, madam: who are you?

MNESILOCHOS:

!

KLEISTHENES:

You, I said. I've got to begin *some*where!

MNESILOCHOS:

!

FIRST WOMAN:

I'll have you know, sir,
my husband's name's Kleónymos.

KLEISTHENES:

Does anyone vouch

49

for Mrs Kleónymos?

CHORAGOS:

Mercy, yes. Known her for years.
Try someone else.

KLEISTHENES:

Who is that fat woman
with the unattractive baby?

FIRST WOMAN:

My nurse, stupid!

MNESILOCHOS:

Well, I must be running along.

KLEISTHENES:

Just a moment, madam.
Where are you off to?

MNESILOCHOS:

Oh sir, spare my blushes . . .
The Little Girls' Room, you know . . .

KLEISTHENES:

Oh. Well, hurry up.

[MNESILOCHOS *moves towards exit, is blocked by the crowd, and conceals himself behind a pillar.*

I'll wait till you come back.

CHORAGOS:

Keep your eye on her.
She's the only woman here that we don't know.

KLEISTHENES:

What's the matter in there? Have you fallen in?

MNESILOCHOS:

                                   Be patient.

You can't imagine, sir, what an obstruction . . .
It must be that cress I ate.

KLEISTHENES:

                        Cress? I'll cress you!

                    [pulls him out from behind pillar:

Come over here!

MNESILOCHOS:

              This is no way to handle
a woman in a delicate condition.

KLEISTHENES:

I want the truth, madam. Who is your husband?

MNESILOCHOS:

Husband? Oh, you mean my husband . . . Why, Whoozis.
From Kothôkidai.

KLEISTHENES:

                 Who's Whoozis?

MNESILOCHOS:

                    Whoozis? He's,
well, Whoozis . . . Son of Whoozis . . . You know . . .

KLEISTHENES:

Sounds evasive to me.

                    —Tell me: Have you ever
been here before?

MNESILOCHOS:

                    Heavens, yes. Every year.

KLEISTHENES:

  Who was your roommate last year?

MNESILOCHOS:

                                    Whoozis was.

KLEISTHENES:

  Madam, I think you lie.

FIRST WOMAN:

                    Step aside, Kleisthenês,
and let me do the questioning. There are some things
a man shouldn't hear.

                    —Now, tell me, you:
What was the opening ceremony last year?

MNESILOCHOS:

  We had a drink.

FIRST WOMAN:

                    And after that?

MNESILOCHOS:

                                    We had
another drink.

FIRST WOMAN:

                    Somebody must have told you.
—Then what happened?

52

MNESILOCHOS:

I remember Xenylla

asked if anyone had a mixing-bowl:

there weren't any chamber-pots.

FIRST WOMAN:

Wrong. Utterly wrong.

—Kleisthenês, here's your man.

KLEISTHENES:

What shall I do?

FIRST WOMAN:

Undress him, naturally.

MNESILOCHOS:

I beg you on my knees,

would you undress the mother of nine sons?

KLEISTHENES:

You revolting reprobate!

FIRST WOMAN:

Strip him, strip him!

—What too too sullied flesh!

KLEISTHENES:

What muscle!

FIRST WOMAN:

What breasts!

They're not in the least like ours.

MNESILOCHOS:

That is because

I have never known the joys of motherhood.

53

FIRST WOMAN:

Well really! What about those nine sons of yours?

KLEISTHENES:

Stop hunching over. Where are you trying to hide
that appendage?

FIRST WOMAN:

Look, it's peeking out behind.
Isn't it cunning?

KLEISTHENES:

Behind? I don't see it.

FIRST WOMAN:

Now it's in front again.

KLEISTHENES:

No.

FIRST WOMAN:

Now it's back here.

KLEISTHENES:

That's a sort of isthmus, friend, between your legs.
It's better travelled than the Korinth Portage.

FIRST WOMAN:

The hateful beast! No wonder he stood up
for Euripides.

MNESILOCHOS:

This is embarrassing.
It's also my own fault.

FIRST WOMAN:

What shall we do now?

KLEISTHENES:

Keep an eye on him. He's slippery. I'm going
to take this business straight to the City Council.

> [*Exit* KLEISTHENES. *Two burly women seize* MNESI-
> LOCHOS *and hustle him to one side of the rostrum,*
> *where he stands guarded.*

CHORIKON:
CHORAL INTERLUDE

CHORAGOS:

Light your lamps, throw off your long cloaks, belt
your tunics tight like men, and search the Pnyx,
the aisles, each corridor, each cell. If another man
is hidden here, he must not get away.

CHORUS:

> Lightly, silently,
> A-tiptoe, swift,
> Dancing the deft search,
> Circle and drift,
> Drift and recircle,
> Rondel and round again,
> Here a man, there a man,
> Catch-as-catch-can a man,
> Left to right, right to left,
> Silently, lightly.

CHORAGOS:

Let the chorus hearten the hunter!

CHORUS:

> If any wretched prying man   [STROPHE
> Is lurking in this place,
> Let him consider, while he can,
> His imminent disgrace.
>
> Let him reflect that Némesis
> Is the bleak wage of error,

59

And let him curse that pride of his
   That brings him down in terror.

His naked punishment shall be
   A paradigm of shame,
And sinners in their infancy
   Shall sicken at his name.

Accurst in living, in his death
   Accurst, beneath all pity,
His tale will not be wasted breath,
   For it shall serve the City,
Proving to each frail citizen
That God will not be mocked. Amen.

AGON: β

CHORAGOS:

We seem to have looked everywhere. It's safe to say
there's not another man in the place.

> [MNESILOCHOS *snatches a baby and takes refuge at*
> *the altar:*

FIRST WOMAN:

>>> Stop thief! Stop thief!

No, over here, look! This filthy old man
has torn my precious babe from its mother's breast.

MNESILOCHOS:

You said it. And you won't feed this brat again
until I get out of here.

> *Sluiced by my steel, the infant blood*
> *Shall dye with its empurpling flood*
> *The holy antependium.*

FIRST WOMAN:

>>> Oh what shall I do?

Friends, friends, will you not help me?
Must I be ravish'd of my only joy?

CHORAGOS:

Arise, black goddesses of vengeance dire!
Have you ever known such an outrage?

FIRST WOMAN:

>>> Dreadful.

SECOND WOMAN:

>>> Horrid.

63

CHORAGOS:

Alas, what more than bloody deed is this?

MNESILOCHOS:

It's simply a method of restoring balance.

SECOND WOMAN:

Makes a woman think twice, a thing like this does.

MNESILOCHOS:

Precisely my motive, Ladies. I *want* you
to think twice.

SECOND WOMAN:

                You barbarian!

FIRST WOMAN:

                      You barefaced
baby-snatcher!

CHORUS: Unblushing monster! Infamy   [ANTISTROPHE
            Incarnate! Beast accurst!
        What tongue can tell your cruelty?
MNESILOCHOS: You've yet to see my worst.

CHORUS: You hope this trick will serve your need?
          You plan to slip away?
       By Heaven, we'll have you fricasseed!
MNESILOCHOS: You're wrong; or so I pray.

CHORUS: Though you invoke celestial Power,
        You'll find no help in that.
      No god descends in a saving shower.

64

MNESILOCHOS: Meanwhile, I have the brat.

CHORUS: Now by the Holy Two I swear,
    Your tide of luck is turning.
Fortune frowns, that once was fair,
    And you are ripe for burning.
The flame that fries your blasphemies
Shall dry this weeping mother's eyes.

CHORAGOS:

Go, some of you, bring lots of wood,
and let's get down to broiling this abomination.

FIRST WOMAN:

A thoroughly sound idea! Manía, get some wood.
—You brute, I'll barbecue you to a crisp.

MNESILOCHOS:

Kindle, parboil, scorch, roast—whatever you say.
It's all the same to me.

               —But you, poor child,
unhappy sacrifice to maternal pigheadedness:
off with these lendings, your tiny
shroud, illstarred darling, and—

                 But what's this?

    [*Fumbling under the wrappings, he has discovered
    only a leather wine-bottle:*

The baby skin you love to touch has become
a dimpling wineskin—yes, with booties attached!

65

O fiery woman, O hydroptic salamander,
marvel of intemperate ingenuity!
These are the tricks that destroy us, bringing
delight to the winemerchant, cobwebs to the hearth,
oblivion to the principles of domestic science.

FIRST WOMAN:

Be sure you stick in plenty of kindling, Manía.

MNESILOCHOS:

Stick it all in.

                   —But first, a question or two.
You assert that this infant is yours?

FIRST WOMAN:

                                 Nine long months
I carried it.

MNESILOCHOS:

               Carried it, eh?

FIRST WOMAN:

                       Yes, by Artemis!

MNESILOCHOS:

How much did it weigh? About a pint and a half?

FIRST WOMAN:

What are you up to? Why, you inhuman pervert,
you've taken its clothes off! It'll catch cold, it's so
teeny-weeny.

MNESILOCHOS:

            Teeny-weeny indeed. How old is it?
Three or four libations, I dare say.

FIRST WOMAN:

About that,

counting from last Dionysia. —Give it back to me.

MNESILOCHOS:

I will not, by Apollo!

FIRST WOMAN:

We'll burn you, then.

MNESILOCHOS:

Burn away. But this innocent must bite the blade.

[*He draws an enormous knife:*

FIRST WOMAN:

I beg you, no! Do with me what you will,

but spare my baby girl!

MNESILOCHOS:

Ah, mother-love!

Nevertheless, this teeny-weeny must bleed.

[*He slashes the bundle. Wine pours out:*

FIRST WOMAN:

My child! My child!

Quick, Manía, pass me the ritual bowl

and let me catch the holy blood of my babe.

MNESILOCHOS:

Hold it lower down. I'll do this much for you.

FIRST WOMAN:

Damn you, you selfish, wasteful he-harlot!

MNESILOCHOS:

To the priestess belongs the victim's tegument.

FIRST WOMAN:

What are you talking about?

MNESILOCHOS:

This. Catch!

[Tosses her the wineskin:

SECOND WOMAN:

O Mika, Mika, what a deflowering!
—Has something happened to your baby, dear?

FIRST WOMAN:

There is the murderer. Ask him.

For that matter,
keep an eye on him while I get Kleisthenês
to make another complaint at Town Hall.   *[Exit*

[The women gather at the rostrum, leaving MNESI-
LOCHOS *alone with his two bored guards.*

MNESILOCHOS:

What exquisite trick, what access of inspiration
will save me now? Come, brain,
excogitate deliverance.

—It was Euripides
got me into this trouble, and where he is now
I do not know. Well, I must send to him.
Yes, but how?

68

              Let me think.
                        He himself
has something in that *Palamedês* of his . . .
A hero in distress
should take an oar and carve the salient facts
on the flat of the blade, and cast it into the sea.

Good. But I have no oar.
There is not a single oar in this sanctuary.
An oar?
            Let's not be bound by precedent.
Why not use one of these votive tablets
hanging on the wall? They're wood; they're flat;
they'll float.

            [*He tears down several wooden plaques from around
            the altar:*

                  O hands of mine, awake!
                  Salvation is at stake!
                  Write! Write!

                        [*He scratches busily with his knife:*
Agh! Literary composition! That infernal R
sprained my wrist.
                  Lie still,
                  Ye missive shingles: feel
                  My incisive chisel chace

                        69

Disgrace upon your face.

That does it! A masterpiece of calligraphy!

[*He hurls the tablets wildly in every direction:*

Depart, be off, I say,
This way, that way, every way,

NORTH

WEST   EAST

SOUTH

Points between:

[*He sits down at the base of the altar:*

End of the *Palamedês* scene.

[*The* CHORUS *turns to face the audience
for the* Parábasis.

PARÁBASIS

CHORAGOS:

The PARÁBASIS at last! A chance to endorse our own praises.

[PARABASIS

—You will hear men, this one and that, dredging up the old lies

About women, calling us the calamity of mankind, the source

Of tiffs, quarrels, sedition, riot, war itself;

Which makes us reflect, sometimes, 'Well, if we're so calamitous,

'Why are you men so fond of marrying calamity?'

And you not only marry it: you keep it hoarded up

In your houses, never letting it so much as stick out its head

For a breath of air. Is this how you cope with calamity?

Or say a poor woman steps out for a moment, and you come home

And find she's gone. What do you do? Rage! Throw things! Kick

The cat! Whereas if you really meant what you say,

You'd be down on your knees praising God and offering up libations

For your happy deliverance from calamity.

Or say

We get bored with all the connubial hilarity and decide

To spend a night or two at a girl friend's house: you

Absurd men crawl under the beds and creep into the closets

73

Looking for calamity. Why, if one of us leans out of a window,
There's a whole platoon of you gawking at calamity,
And when she pops back in, overcome by all this attention,
You can hardly wait until calamity reappears.

It seems probable, then, that there's something about us you
    like.

You say we're the frail sex. We say you are. Well, let's exam-
    ine
The evidence. It might be useful to begin with our names.
'Victoria' is better than 'Elmer', you can hardly deny that,
And 'Gaby' is clearly more delicious than 'John Thomas',
And it's been a long time since any of you men have dared
Stand up to a 'Gloria'; and as for 'Prudence',
Is there a single Assemblyman in the whole roster
Who can look her in the eye? After that meeting last year,
Even you would be ashamed. The frail sex? You don't see
    women
Embezzling thousands out of the public funds and then riding
Around town bragging about the friends they've bought.
It takes a man to do that. No, when we women steal,
It's some little tiny thing, maybe a peck of wheat or so,
And we steal it from our own husbands; and you'll find
We more than pay it back the very day it was stolen.

      Can you say as much for yourselves? What   [MAKRON
      Dinner-table strategists you are, what

74

Suave operators, crumbsnatchers, what
Gifted exploiters of slaves! (They're more
Helpless—aren't they?—than women.)
We know about warping and woofing, we
Know where our pots and pans are. You
Men, can you lay your hands on
Any essentially male implement—
A spear, say, or a buckler? No.
You've mislaid it; or you threw it
Away on some battlefield.

[EPIRRHEMA

Complaints against you? We have many, but one's
Particularly important: the way you treat us in public.
Surely the woman who produces a valuable son—
A general or a top sergeant—should be honoured by the State.
She should have a special place at the Stênia
And the Skira and all the other public festivals.
Similarly, if it's a coward she's borne, some
Navy grafter or some incompetent pilot,
They should give her a salad-bowl haircut and make her sit
In the back row. It's a scandal, a civic disgrace,
To seat brave Lamachos's mother side by side
With Hypérbolos's, that awful woman with her white gown
And her silly hair-do, financing cheap deals
At outrageous rates! Rates? She should get
No interest at all from anyone fool enough

75

To deal with her. She ought to be confiscated,
Frozen, immobilized, with the notation:
'No interest allowed for your interesting son.'

[*The* CHORUS *resumes its place.*

SCENE

MNESILOCHOS:

This waiting for Euripides
has got me cross-eyed. Where can he be?
Maybe his *Palamedês*
bores him now. I should think it would.
Which one of his plays will bring him, I wonder?
I have it! I'll try that new hit of his,
the *Helen*. At any rate, I'm dressed for the part.

SECOND WOMAN:

What are you up to now? What are you batting
them big brown eyes at me for? You behave,
or you'll get Helen all right when the Chief comes.

MNESILOCHOS:

All hail, ye virgin waves of Nilus' flood,
Hail, holy stream, that with moist inundation
Dost annually drench white Ægypt's sod
And dosify with black th' Ægyptian nation!

SECOND WOMAN:

In the name of Hekatê, what's the matter with you?

MNESILOCHOS:

Sparta my native land, no óbscure soil;
Old Tyndareus the father is of me.

SECOND WOMAN:

He is, is he? Old Phrynôndas, more likely.

MNESILOCHOS:

Helen my name—

SECOND WOMAN:

Listen, are you turning
woman on us again? You aren't through paying
for the first time.

MNESILOCHOS:

—*and all for love of me*
On sad Skamandrian strand braw heroes died.

SECOND WOMAN:

It's a damn pity you didn't die yourself.

MNESILOCHOS:

Here lost and lorn I lope, and Menelaos,
My hapless husband, cometh not to me.
He cometh not, I say. Why then, alas,
Do I persist in living?

SECOND WOMAN:

That's a fair question.

MNESILOCHOS:

But what sweet vision swims into my ken?
Delusive God, mock not my hopeful heart!

[*Enter* EURIPIDES *in dripping rags tangled with seaweed:*

EURIPIDES:

What prince inhabits this impressive pile?
Speak: of his courtesy will he provide
For mariners shipwrack'd on the salt sea?

80

MNESILOCHOS:

'Tis *Prôteus rules these rafters.*

SECOND WOMAN:

You're a liar!

Protéas has been dead a good ten years.

EURIPIDES:

What realm is this to which my barque hath come?

MNESILOCHOS:

'Tis *Ægypt, sire.*

EURIPIDES:

Alack, how have I strayed!

SECOND WOMAN:

Friend, you mustn't believe a thing this fool
tells you. This here's the Thesmophorion.

EURIPIDES:

Lord Prôteus, is he within, or is he without?

SECOND WOMAN:

You must be still feeling the sea, stranger.
I just got through saying Protéas is dead.

EURIPIDES:

'Las, is he dead? Where then is his sepulchre?

MNESILOCHOS:

This is his tomb upon the which I park.

SECOND WOMAN:

Well, I'll be damned! And so will you, damn you,
calling this here altar a damn tomb!

EURIPIDES:

O thou adorning this sarcophagus,
Tell me, why is thy visage thus enveil'd?

MNESILOCHOS:

Th' insensate force of local circumstance
Drives me to share the couch of Prôteus' son.

SECOND WOMAN:

You ought to be ashamed of yourself, you should so,
to lie like this to a stranger.

                       —Look, friend,

this son of a bitch broke in here this morning
to pick us women's pockets.

MNESILOCHOS:

                      Base yelping brach,
On me discharge the venom of thy hate!

EURIPIDES:

Damsel, what hag is this accuseth thee?

MNESILOCHOS:

'Tis Prôteus' daughter, the Lady Theonoê.

SECOND WOMAN:

Now this is a little too much. I'll have you know
my name's Kritylla, just plain Kritylla,
and my old man's name was Antitheos, by God,
and we hail from Gargettos. And you're a bastard.

MNESILOCHOS:

Rail as thou wilt, I will not wed thy bro.,
Nor fail my Troyan Menelaos so.

82

EURIPIDES:

Soft, soft! What word is this assails mine ears?

Oh turn on me those orbs enlakèd in tears!

MNESILOCHOS:

I blush to shew thee my revilèd face,

But natheless—

EURIPIDES:

                Angels and ministers of grace!

What eye is this I eye? 'Tis praeterhuman!

My brain swoons with surmise. Who art thou, woman?

MNESILOCHOS:

Nay, who art thou? My symptoms are the same.

EURIPIDES:

Art thou a Hellene, or indigenous dame?

MNESILOCHOS:

A Hellene. And thou, stranger, what thy race?

EURIPIDES:

Lady, on thee detect I Helen's face?

MNESILOCHOS:

And Menelaos' I on thee? I know,

Because thy vegetation tells me so.

EURIPIDES:

In sooth, thou contemplat'st that wretched wretch.

MNESILOCHOS:

To thee my wifely arms do I outstretch.

Oh hold me, hold me, hold me in thine own!

Come let me kiss thee, making murm'rous moan,

And let us then be going, going, gone!

SECOND WOMAN:

Any going going on around this place

is going to get a touch of this torch of mine.

EURIPIDES:

Yea, is't e'en so? Wouldst thou keep Tyndar's daughter
From the bed and board her legal husband brought her?

SECOND WOMAN:

I get it now. You're in this plot too,

you and that talk about Egypt. I might have known.

Well, he'll get what's coming to him, all the same.

Here's the Chief now.

[*Enter* MAGISTRATE *with an oafish* POLICEMAN:

EURIPIDES (*apart, to* MNESILOCHOS):

That play of mine, it seems,

Failed to work out. Ah well, we tried!

I think I'd better be going.

MNESILOCHOS:

What about me?

EURIPIDES:

There's nothing whatever for you to worry about.

Not while I live

shall it be said that I abandoned you.

I've still a trick or two up this sleeve of mine.

MNESILOCHOS:

Yes. But this last trick buttered few parsnips.

[*Exit* EURIPIDES

84

MAGISTRATE:

Is this the rapist that Kleisthenês reported?

SECOND WOMAN:

It is, your Worship.

MAGISTRATE:

H'm. Typical.

Notice he can't meet my eyes.

—Very good.

Officer, take this prisoner inside,

tie him to a plank, bring him out and prop him up.

Do you understand me?

POLICEMAN:

Yass, Marse Chief.

MAGISTRATE:

And guard him with your life, Officer.

If his accomplices attempt a rescue,

remember to use your whip.

POLICEMAN:

I use it, yass.

SECOND WOMAN:

Goodness knows he may have to! Just now

there was some sort of travelling salesman here

trying to spring him.

MNESILOCHOS:

Commissioner, by that eager

palm of yours, I implore you:

Grant me a favour, since sentence has been passed.

MAGISTRATE:

What favour, fellow?

MNESILOCHOS:

                    Before your associate
attaches me to the plank that you have mentioned,
have him strip me naked. If carrion crows must eat me,
it would be wrong to spoil their meal with the sight
of this saffron gown.

MAGISTRATE:

                    Denied. The Court has ruled
that you must suffer in your peculiar gear.

MNESILOCHOS:

Absurdly decked, must I absurdly die?

                    [*Exit* MAGISTRATE

Alas, I am a saffron mockery.

        [*The* POLICEMAN *and the Guards take* MNESILOCHOS
        inside.

HYPÓRCHEMA: DANCE SONG

CHORAGOS:

The dance, the women's dance, at the holy hour
When the Two Goddesses lead the solemn games,
    And Pausôn himself, starved, dry,
        Burns to multiply
The rigours of fasting for ever in their names.

      Whirl, whirl in a round
  Follow the beat
        of the clever feet,
    And whirl, hand
        circling hand
  body bent to the sweet
      strict saraband:

CHORUS:

      Sing for the gods   [STROPHE Iα
    Olympian deathless Sing
Timeless hours in the lyric rage of the dance

      No woman's tongue   -   [STROPHE Iβ
    Contrive in this ritual
A word of hate for any hateful man

      All our art   [ANTISTROPHE I
    Draw the mystical round
Of the central Awe the cyclic Mystery

I dance in the name   [STROPHE II
Of Apollo: O Music!
I dance in the name
Of Artemis: chaste Archer!
      Defence from afar!
I dance in the name
Of Hêra: Bride Goddess!
      Guardian of Marriage!
      Join my dance.

I dance in the name   [ANTISTROPHE II
Of Hermês: O Shepherd!
I dance in the name
Of Pan and all Nymphs:
      May they attend us!
I dance the women's dance,
The circle recircled,
      In this holy season:
      Join my dance.

CHORAGOS:

  Iô Bacchos

      Coronal of ivy

           Wild Master

     Leap for us

  Lead us

      Spin for us in the dance

CHORUS:

      Descend O child of Sémelê thou   [STROPHE III
         Tumultuous Flame
O son of Zeus come down upon us now
         —Evion evion evohé!—
         In song cascading
From hills where the Maenads chant Dionysos' name:

      Kithairon shudders with music a shout [ANTISTROPHE III
         Bursts from the stone
The upland thickets howl in the nymphic rout
         —Evion evion evohé!—
         Of the cortège advancing
As the smitten god strides on to join the dancing.

SCENE

[*Rëenter* POLICEMAN *and Guards carrying* MNESILO-CHOS *bound to a large plank, which they deposit at the foot of the altar.*

POLICEMAN:

Sure and it's all outdoors you got now
to screech in.

MNESILOCHOS:

I implore you, Lieutenant—

POLICEMAN:

No soap.

MNESILOCHOS:

Prithee undo this knot.

POLICEMAN:

Knot? Yass.

MNESILOCHOS:

Confound your incompetence, you're making it
tighter!

POLICEMAN:

More tight, Boss?

MNESILOCHOS:

Ouch!

POLICEMAN:

Yass?

MNESILOCHOS:

You're killing me.

POLICEMAN:

                    Yerra, make up your mind!
—Now you wait here, Boss. I go in and get
Soft seat to sit on. I come right back.   [*Exit*

MNESILOCHOS:

This is the persuasive art of Euripides,
and you can have it.

                    [*He looks offstage, startled*:

                    —But what's this I see?
Almighty everlasting Zeus, it's Euripides
himself! He has come back! He would not leave me
desolate, forsaken, but returns disguised
as Perseus; and from the signs that he is making,
I must play Andrómeda. Well, I'm chained tight enough.
I will be Andrómeda, and thus I begin
my girlish lamentation:

            [*The following aria is accompanied by sporadic musi-
            cal effects offstage.* MNESILOCHOS' *singing wavers
            unpredictably between treble and bass:*

Ye dolorous maids, ye virgins, coronal
Of my bright days enduskèd now in doom,
O playmates mine: Behold me now
Reject,.
            abject,
                    disject,
The object of a vile policeman's whim.

96

O Echo, Echo,
Dost hear me in thy cavernous concave?
Speak, Nymph: wilt thou show
Compassion, damn it all, and send me home
To my poor wife?

        (Yea, woman's life
        Is hard, but far harder
        The heart of my warder.)

Girlish coëvals, quondam confidantes mine,
Is it for this I have engulphed the wiles
Of antic harlots at their festival?
Is there to be no quiring hymeneal,
No sweet prothalamy, for wretched me?
Rigid, rapt
On this slivery joist,
No true-love knot adorning, but loveless
Links and buckles bite my nubile limbs,
Pure virgin meat, more meet for clasp
Less cruel!
        And Glauketês,
Remorseless fish,
Lurks, lurks i' the wave, a monster moist,
To maul my shrinking flesh.

I am the most unhappy man that ever lived.

O all ye Nymphs that pass by on the road,
Sing me no nuptial lay, but a threne, a threne,
Beating your bright breasts.

                                A maiden's curse
On the inhuman cad that ruined me,
Shaved me, plucked me, left me in saffron gown
To suffer at the pleasure of this select
Sorority!

                    Yet who can bend the Fates?
No, rather the daystar sag from the firmament
And solar rage encrisp me to a turn!
Then, as I burn,
I'll wind my lamentable neck in death
And pass away on a melodious breath.

                    [*The voice of* EURIPIDES *is heard offstage:*

EURIPIDES:

Greetings, fair Princess; but a malediction
on the unnatural parent who staked you out
here on the rocks.

MNESILOCHOS:

                                Whose is the voice I hear?

EURIPIDES:

Echo I'm called, Echo, illusive nymph
yielding antiphonies to human speech.
This wild strand knows me well: a year ago
I performed here for Euripides.

98

                                        —But you,
Lady Andrómeda, have you learned your lines?
Begin with a groan.

MNESILOCHOS:

                            You will groan after me?

EURIPIDES:

Groan for groan and grunt for grunt. I swear it.

> [*In the following passage* EURIPIDES' *voice, as off-*
> *stage echo, should be different in timbre and much*
> *louder than the phrases echoed:*

MNESILOCHOS:

O holy Night,
Along the bright
Starspangled aether how slow thy flight!
Thy car celest,
Proceeding west,
Caresseth high Olympos's breast.

EURIPIDES:

                            PUSSY'S BREAST!

MNESILOCHOS:

Is this the price
A virgin nice
Must pay for connubial surmise?

EURIPIDES:

                            HER MICE!

MNESILOCHOS:

O Fate inexorable!—

EURIPIDES:

BULL!

MNESILOCHOS:

For God's sake, stop your chattering!

EURIPIDES:

AT A RING?

MNESILOCHOS:

Damn you, can't you see I'm busy?

EURIPIDES:

IS HE?

MNESILOCHOS:

How can I render a Euripidean monody
if you keep on talking?

EURIPIDES:

KEEP ON TALKING!

MNESILOCHOS:

Damn you!

EURIPIDES:

AND YOU!

MNESILOCHOS:

Is there no hope?

EURIPIDES:

NOPE!

MNESILOCHOS:

I despair—

100

EURIPIDES:

I'D A SPARE—

MNESILOCHOS:

I stutter—

EURIPIDES:

ICED UDDER!

MNESILOCHOS:

Woe, woe!

EURIPIDES:

WHOA!

MNESILOCHOS:

I'm a wretch!

EURIPIDES:

I'M A-RETCH!

[Reënter POLICEMAN *with a footstool:*

POLICEMAN:

Who you talk to?

EURIPIDES:

YOU TALK, TOO!

POLICEMAN:

You get funny, yass?

EURIPIDES:

FUNNY ASS!

MNESILOCHOS:

God no, Officer! It's this woman.

EURIPIDES:

HIS WOMAN!

POLICEMAN:

I no see woman.

EURIPIDES:

NOSY WOMAN!

POLICEMAN:

You son of bitch, I find you!

EURIPIDES:

BEHIND YOU!

POLICEMAN:

Where that woman?

MNESILOCHOS:

Seems to have gone now.

POLICEMAN:

Boss, that woman talk too much.

> [EURIPIDES *suddenly appears suspended over their heads by entirely visible wires. He is in the costume of Perseus—winged sandals and helmet—and carries a shield emblazoned with the head of the Cheshire Cat.*

EURIPIDES:

What alien shore is this, ye gods, upon
The which my rapid sandal doth descend?
Cleaving the vast inane, I hasten on
To Argos with this Gorgon head in hand.

POLICEMAN:

What you say, Chief? You got Marse Gorgos' haid?

EURIPIDES:

The Gorgon's head, vile varlet!

POLICEMAN:

Yass. That Gorgos.

EURIPIDES:

But stay! Upon these cruel rocks a rich
And maiden form is drapèd in distress!
As men a dory to a mooring hitch,
So hitch'd is she by cables merciless.

MNESILOCHOS:

Stranger, in Pity's name I thee conjúre:
Dissolve my bondage.

POLICEMAN:

Pretty funny, yass.
You damn fool, Boss: you talk too much too late.

EURIPIDES:

Virgin supine, I see and pity thee.

POLICEMAN:

Him a virgin? That old goat? Ha!

EURIPIDES:

Barb'rous dog,
'Tis Kêpheus' girl, Andrómed, that thou doggest.

POLICEMAN:

Girl, yass? She got big ramming machine.

103

EURIPIDES:

Give me thy white hand, lady.

POLICEMAN:

No!

EURIPIDES:

Officer,

as man to man: each one of us

has his own little weaknesses, don't you find?

Well, mine is a sudden and desperate passion for

this radiant maiden.

POLICEMAN:

You got funny taste, Chief.

I turn him over, yass? and you do your stuff.

EURIPIDES:

For me t' unbind her, churl, it were more meet,
And then to gambol on the nuptial sheet.

POLICEMAN:

You bet. You want to lay this old bastard,

you go right ahead. I no object.

EURIPIDES:

Nay, by Heav'n,

I'll loose those loops!

POLICEMAN:

Not while I got this whip.

EURIPIDES:

Aroint thee!

104

POLICEMAN:

Go to hell!

EURIPIDES:

Alas the day,
What argument will melt this brutish clay?
Yea, what avails the honey tongue of sense
To lick the sap of impercipience?
Some other circumventing means must I
Devise to combat the gendarmerie.　　　　　　　　　*[Exit*

POLICEMAN:

That old fox think he make monkey out of me.

MNESILOCHOS:

Perseus, remember me,
A maid betrothèd to adversity!

POLICEMAN:

Silence in the court! You see this whip?

> [MNESILOCHOS *subsides; the* POLICEMAN *sits down upon his stool and immediately falls asleep.*

105

CHORIKON:
CHORAL INTERLUDE

CHORAGOS:

I call upon Pallas. Hear me, Goddess!

CHORUS:

Maiden peerless, Lover   [STROPHE I
  Of choric song, descend:
Thou Keeper of the City's keys,
  Almighty Friend!

CHORAGOS:

I call upon Pallas, Destroyer of Tyranny.

CHORUS:

Warrior Virgin, Patron   [ANTISTROPHE I
  Of Athens town, be near:
To women suppliant incline
  Thy gracious ear.

And the two august Ladies whose ritual   [STROPHE II
  We sing today,
Let them send down a benison to fall
  On us at play.
    Here no male insolence
      Dares violate
   The holy ground whose awful innocence
      We consecrate.

Hear us, O Goddesses! If as of old   [ANTISTROPHE II
  You mark our prayer,
Flame down in radiance twofold

From the bright air.
Come, O Persephonê,
Deméter, come!
The sacred dance with double instancy
Summons you home.

ÉXODOS

[*Reënter* EURIPIDES, *dressed as in the Prologue, carrying a lyre. He is accompanied by a boy fluteplayer and a nearly naked dancing-girl.*]

EURIPIDES:

Ladies, I have a proposal to make to you.

If you are concerned, as I am,
to make an end to this lamentable feud,
I promise, for my part, never again to write
or speak any ill of women.

CHORAGOS:

               That is handsome.
But why this change of heart?

EURIPIDES:

               The gentleman
attached to the plank there is my father-in-law.
He is my motive. Release him, and you and I
are friends for ever. Refuse, and I
will publish every naughty secret you have
when your husbands come back home.

CHORAGOS:

               Fair enough,
so far as we are concerned. But you'll have to persuade
this constable.

EURIPIDES:

           That should be no problem.

Look, Fleurette: [*to the dancing-girl:*

Do you remember what you're supposed to do?
Dance over in front of him, give him
a waggle or two, and dance back.

                       —You, Terêdôn,
let's have a Persian polka on your flute.

> [*While the girl is dancing,* EURIPIDES *disguises him-
> self as an old woman. Near the end of the dance the*
> POLICEMAN *wakes up.*

POLICEMAN:

Sweet moosics do I hear?

                    —What is this? A
floor show, yass?

EURIPIDES:

                Sir, we beg your pardon.
This little lady has been engaged to dance
at a big convention down town, and we stopped here
for a kind of rehearsal.

POLICEMAN:

                Is O.K. by me.
Maybe you let me rehearse her too?
How quick she wiggle, like a flea in the whiskers!

EURIPIDES:

Your dress, Fleurette, your dress! Slip it off,
do.
     There.

Now sit down on the gentleman's knee,
and I'll unstrap your sandals.

POLICEMAN:

Yass, sit down,
Baby, and I unstrap too.

—Oh the little tits,
all stiff, round, yass, like little parsnips!

EURIPIDES:

Pick up the tempo, Terêdôn.

—Fleurette,
don't tell me you're bashful with this gentleman!

POLICEMAN:

And a tight little ass, yass.

I feel
funny, like I want something.

EURIPIDES:

I'm sure you do, sir.
—That's all, Fleurette. Put your dress back on.
It's getting late.

POLICEMAN:

Maybe she kiss me, lady?

EURIPIDES:

Kiss the gentleman, Fleurette.

POLICEMAN:

My God, a sweet kiss!
Oh little tongue, so good, so curly, like

Attika honey.

—Maybe she sleep with me?

POLICEMAN:

EURIPIDES:

Really, sir, there are certain things
that—

POLICEMAN:

No, no, lady. I pay. I pay good!

EURIPIDES:

A drachma, say?

POLICEMAN:

One drachma, yass.

EURIPIDES:

Let me see
your money.

POLICEMAN:

Lady, I have no money.
I give you this belt.

[*He unbuckles his belt and hands it to* EURIPIDES.
Then, to the girl:
—Now you come.

—Lady,
how you call her?

EURIPIDES:

Her name is Artemisia.

POLICEMAN:

Hattie Mischa? I got it.

116

—You come now, Hattie Mischa.

[*Exit* POLICEMAN *with the girl.* EURIPIDES *strips off his disguise.*

EURIPIDES:

A job well done, I swear by Hermês the Diddler!

—That's all, Terêdôn. You can go. And take this lyre.

—Now to the rescue.

—Father-in-law,
now that you're free, I advise you to make tracks
for your inconsolable wife and your little ones.

MNESILOCHOS:

You advise right.

EURIPIDES:

There's the last rope! Now let's get going
before the policeman comes back here.

MNESILOCHOS:

You said it.

[*Exeunt*

[*Reënter* POLICEMAN *solus, dishevelled:*

POLICEMAN:

Lady, I thank you for little girl. She real nice,
she not so slow!

—Lady? Where old lady go?

117

I smell mouse.

—And old man? He go too?

I been buggered!

—Old lady? Old lady?

This not very nice of you.

—You, Hattie Mischa?

Yerra, where is old lady? Hattie Mischa?

She fix me up, all right.

[*Seeing his discarded belt on the ground, and kicking it:*

Yass,

and you, you son of bitch, you sure

belt me one in the bushes! You go to hell!

Ladies, where is old lady?

CHORAGOS:

You refer, sir,

to the respectable person with the harp?

POLICEMAN:

Yass'm, you bet.

[CHORAGOS *points in wrong direction:*

CHORAGOS:

She went that way,

and there was an elderly gentleman with her.

POLICEMAN:

He have saffron dress on?

CHORAGOS:

Now that you mention it,
I believe he did. If you hurry you may catch them.

POLICEMAN:

This way they go? This way?

—You, Hattie Mischa!

CHORAGOS:

No. Not that way. Over there.

—Really, sir,
you'll get nowhere running around in circles.

POLICEMAN:

Yass, I run in circles, but I go!
—Hey, Hattie Mischa!

[*Exit in the wrong direction*

CHORAGOS:

Go, and hell take you!

[*to the audience:*

—Friends:
It is late, and our play is done. Let us all
go quietly home and pray the Goddesses
grant us their blessing at this Festival.

GENERAL NOTES
AND
INDEX OF PROPER NAMES

GENERAL NOTES

Σ = Scholiast

Page

xii: *Persons Represented*: Mnesilochos is nowhere named in the play, and the textual evidence for his name is contradictory. Σ says, 'Mnesilochos prologuizes,' and identifies him as a κηδεστής— that is to say, a relative by marriage—of Euripides. I have followed a venerable but suspect tradition in making him the poet's father-in-law.

3: *'If winter comes', they say*: The Greek proverb is, 'When will the swallow come back?'

3: In the opening lines of the play A. is making fun of the metaphysical jargon of the Sophists, with whom he (more or less unfairly) associates Euripides.

4: *to become suddenly lame*: Then he would not have to walk at all.

9: *I libel them*: This was certainly Euripides' reputation, although such plays as *Alkêstis* and *The Trojan Women* should have been enough to offset the misogyny of the *Hippolytos, Medea,* and (presumably) the lost *Melanippê*. It should be said, however, that even Euripides' virtuous women have a Cordelia-like inhumanity.

10: *assemble with the Assembly*: No men were admitted, of course.

10: *you take the cake*: Already proverbial in A.'s time.

12: *in the style of Aischylos*: Mnesilochos cites the Lykourgian Tetralogy of Aischylos (now lost), where, in the second play,

123

King Lykourgos is impudently questioning the god Dionysos, not knowing who he is. It is the effeminate manner and dress of Dionysos, like Agathôn's, that gives the travesty its point.

15: *Brevity . . . is the soul of wit*: The original cites two lines from the (lost) *Aiolos* of Euripides.

16: *'You love the sun . . .'*: Quoted from the *Alkêstis* of Euripides (691).

18: *Off with that cloak*: Σ says that this depilation scene is 'taken' from a comedy (variously called *Idaioi* and *Empipramenoi*) by Kratinos.

24: *it is your heart, and not your tongue*: This famous evasion, from the *Hippolytos* of Euripides, seems to have amused A. particularly. He cites it again, with crushing effect, near the end of *The Frogs*. In the original, of course, it was the tongue, and not the heart, that swore.

25: The *Párodos,* or Entrance of the Chorus, brings us into the Temple where the Festival of the Thesmophoria is being celebrated. The liturgical passages that follow are of considerable interest because they parody or imitate ritual formulas and practices of which little is actually known. A formal invocation in prose is followed by a more extended one in verse, which I have cast in the form of a Litany; and this, in turn, passes into a Ritual Cursing of the kind that may still be found in the Anglican Service of Commination, prescribed for Ash Wednesday. These curses are summarized in a rather perfunctory concluding hymn, and the business of the meeting follows immediately.

28: *Givers of Law*: The dual number is used, for the Givers of Law are Deméter and her daughter Persephonê. The Festival is called *Thesmophoria* after them in this aspect (Θεσμοφόρω). It was a three-day feast, celebrated in November; and in this play we have arrived at the Second Day, *Nêsteia,* which is given over to fasting and secret business. The mysteries are inviolable, and consequently the invasion of them by a man is a scandal of horrifying proportions.

30: *consort with the Persians*: The warning against treason was a part of the regular ritual; the warning against Euripides is a part of the parody.

36: *the vegetable dealer's son*: A. is never tired of asserting that the mother of Euripides, Kleitô, sold greens for a living.

37: *'th' adult'rous guest'*: The allusion is to the *Stheneboia,* a (lost) tragedy by Euripides, but it is so contorted that I have tried to render it by a paratragic line. The sense is that a guilty wife, thinking of her lover, drops a pitcher and breaks it.

37: *'morning greenness'*: Euripidean parody again, but of an unknown source. A brother notices with suspicion that his sister is inclined to be unwell at breakfast-time.

37: *'What's wedlock . . .'*: From the (lost) *Phoinix* of Euripides.

39: *brought up on wild vegetables*: See note on p. 36, *supra.*

44: *the proverb says*: It says 'Under every stone there's a scorpion.' A. substitutes 'orator' for 'scorpion': a frigid joke, though not so frigid as my rendering of it.

46: *chopped her husband up*: Σ refers to Klytaimnestra, who murdered her husband Agamemnon.

48: *mad about women*: That is to say, he wants to resemble women; he is a pathic. —A. invents a verb, γυναικομανῶ; so in *The Birds,* ὀρνιθομανῶ: 'I'm bird-crazy'.

51: *Whoozis*: Mnesilochos keeps repeating τὸν δεῖνα, just as we say 'Whaddyacallum', and the Spaniards 'Fulano'.

54: *that appendage*: Mnesilochos is wearing, and concealing with increasing difficulty, the prominent ritual *phallos.*

63: *has torn my precious babe*: The first woman, providing against the austerities of the Day of Fasting, has wrapped up a wineskin in baby clothes and brought it to the Assembly. A. is fond of the idea that the women of Athens are too much given to drink.

67: *counting from last Dionysia*: That is to say, seven months.

69: *that* Palamedês *of his*: The *Palamedês* of Euripides was one of a trilogy performed in 415 B.C., the two other tragedies being *Alexandros* and *The Trojan Women,* with *Sisyphos* as satyr-play. Of these only *The Trojan Women* has survived. Palamedês himself, a Greek chieftain in the Trojan War, was murdered at Troy: 'and Euripides shows in [this play],' says Σ, 'how Palamedês' brother Oiax . . . wrote an account of the death on several oar blades and cast them into the sea', in order that one of them might carry the news to their father Nauplios.

71: *Parábasis*: At this point the action is suspended and the poet addresses the audience through the Chorus. As a dramatic form, a *parábasis* has a rather complicated structure; but it was subject to change (and even to omission), and in this play it is severely curtailed.

79: *the* Helen: The *Helen* of Euripides was produced in 412 B.C., the year before our comedy. In it the dramatist accepts the counter-myth, recorded by Herodotos and others, that Helen was not taken to Troy by Paris, but to Egypt, where she was impounded (as it were) by the kindly King Proteus, and later retrieved by her husband Menelaos. (The Helen at Troy was only an *imago* of her, a phantom of delight.) Aristophanes' delightful recognition scene is a masterpiece of friendly parody.

81: *Protéas has been dead*: The sentry woman, Kritylla, has never heard of King Proteus of Egypt, and confuses the name with that of one Protéas—an Athenian citizen, presumably, of whom we know nothing, nor is it necessary that we should.

81: *What realm is this*: Menelaos, returning from Troy with his wife—or the phantom of his wife, although he does not know this—, has been blown to the shore of Egypt, where he is startled to find a counter-wife, the real Helen, seated upon the royal tomb.

84: *a . . . POLICEMAN*: The ordinary Athenian policeman was a

Skythian archer. A. makes this one speak a barbarous, though by no means consistent, dialect or perversion of Greek. The translation pushes this to an extreme: I had in mind a Comedy Cop, minstrel-show blackface with bright red hair, a surrealist nightmare of jargon.

96: *I will be Andrómeda*: The *Andrómeda* of Euripides, now lost, was produced in 412 B.C. This time Aristophanes' parody seems more cruel: the heroine's pathetic monody, with the graceful echo device, is reduced to utter absurdity; and the interpolations of the Policeman, a caricature of the sea-monster Glauketês, are a devastating final touch.

111: *Exodos*: The resolution of comedy is perfunctory enough: the sudden agreement between Euripides and the Chorus is improbable, to say the least, and one feels that A. is looking for the quickest and easiest way to make an end of the business. Plot, however, is of minor importance in most of A.'s compositions, the *Lysistrata* being a notable exception.

116: *this belt*: In the original he hands over his quiver, an essential part of his equipment; and this produces, a few lines later, an indelicate pun that can not be taken over directly into English. 'Belt' makes a less explosive pun possible.

INDEX OF PROPER NAMES

AGATHON: Dramatist, dilettante in arts and philosophy; satirized frequently by A. for his affected manner and supposed effeminacy; *fl.* 406 B.C.

AGLAUROS: One of the three daughters of Kekrôps, King of Athens, the other two being Pandrosos and Hersê. Σ says that it was customary to swear 'by Aglauros!' or 'by Pandrosos!', but never 'by Hersê!'

AISCHYLOS, AESCHYLUS: Tragic poet (525-456 B.C.)

ALKAIOS: Lyric poet (*fl. c.* 600 B.C.)

ANDROMEDA: Daughter of King Kepheus of Ethiopia. Her father, guided by an oracle, had her chained to the base of a seaside cliff and left to the mercy of a sea monster, Glauketês. She was rescued by Perseus, who later married her. She is the heroine of the *Andromeda* of Euripides, a play produced in 412 B.C. and now lost.

APOLLO: God of the sun.

ARGOS: An ancient city of the Peloponnesos, capital of Argolis.

ARTEMIS: Goddess of the hunt and of virgins; sister of Apollo.

ATHENA: Goddess of wisdom, tutelary divinity of Athens.

BACCHOS: A name for Dionysos, god of wine.

DELOS: An island, one of the Cyclades; birthplace of Apollo and Artemis, hence called DELIAN.

DEMETER: The earth-goddess, mother of PERSEPHONE, *q.v.;* see also GENERAL NOTES for p. 28.

DIONYSIA: Festivals of the god DIONYSOS, *q.v.* The reference in line 747 is to the most important of these, the City Dionysia, celebrated at the end of March, seven months before the Thesmophoria.

DIONYSOS: God of wine; also patron god of dramatists and the theatre.

ECHO: An attendant of Hêra who seems to have played Hedda Gabler to Zeus's Ejlert Løvborg. She betrayed Zeus's amorous secrets to his wife, and was punished by being deprived of the power of spontaneous speech. See GENERAL NOTES for p. 96.

EURIPIDES: Tragic poet (484-406 B.C.)

GARGETTOS: A suburb north-east of Athens.

GLAUKETES: A sea monster; *see* ANDROMEDA.

GORGON: Any one of three incredible sisters, daughters of Phorkys and Kêtô, who were golden-winged, brass-handed and serpent-haired. The only mortal among them was Medûsa, whose face had the power to turn beholders to stone. She was killed by Perseus, *q.v.*, who cut off her head and carried it with him as a useful weapon in combat.

GORGOS: Apparently an *ad hoc* name. The Policeman has never heard of the GORGON, *q.v.*, and comes up with a name that sounds something like.

GRACES: Thaleia, Euphrosynê and Aglaia, daughters of Zeus (or Dionysos) and Aphroditê.

HEKATE: Generally, a goddess of witchcraft; assimilated to several other deities, as Selênê in heaven, Artemis on earth, and Persephonê in Hadês; hence represented as *Triformis* (with three bodies) or *Triceps* (with three heads). Understandably, a favourite oath among women.

HELENA, HELEN: Daughter of Zeus by Lêda, Queen of Sparta (King Tyndareus being the nominal father); wife of MENELAOS, *q.v.*;

seduced and abducted by Paris, a Prince of Troy, she was made the pretext for the Trojan War. See GENERAL NOTES for p. 79.

HELLENE: Greek.

HERA: Sister and wife of ZEUS, *q.v.*

HERMES: The messenger-god.

HIPPOKRATES: An unpopular Athenian notable, a nephew of Periklês. His sons were popularly known as 'the swine of Hippokratês': hence the 'sty' in verse 273.

HYPERBOLOS: A corrupt politician and soldier, recently dead, whose mother seems to have made herself unpopular by lending money at exorbitant rates.

IBYKOS: Lyric poet (*fl. c.* 540 B.C.).

KALLIGENEIA: 'She who brings forth beauty': an epithet for both DE-METER and PERSEPHONE, *qq.v.*; later dissociated from the goddesses and made a spirit (δαίμων) attendant upon Deméter [Σ].

KEPHEUS: A king of Ethiopia; father of ANDROMEDA, *q.v.*

KITHAIRON: A mountain in Boiotia, near Thebes.

KLEISTHENES: A beardless, effeminate person [Σ] frequently satirized by A.; his function here is that of a Women's Advocate (πρόξενος), and Rogers' note is worth repeating: 'So thoroughly is he identified with the womankind, that the Chorus express no indignation at his appearance amongst them.'

KLEONYMOS: A corrupt politician, a cowardly soldier, a shameless informer, a favourite butt of A.'s scorn.

KORINTH: A city on the isthmus between Attika and the Peloponnesos.

KOTHOKIDES: A town of uncertain location.

KYPROS, CYPRUS: A large island in the Mediterranean off the coast of Syria.

KYRENE: An accomplished and notorious prostitute.

LAMACHOS: An Athenian general killed at Syracuse on the Sicilian Expedition (414 B.C.). A. had once lampooned him cruelly, but treats him now with deserved respect.

LETO: A daughter of Kronos; mother, by Zeus, of APOLLO and ARTEMIS, *qq.v.*

MAENAD: One of the train of frenzied women attendant upon DIONYSOS, *q.v.*

MELANIPPE: Heroine of one of the lost tragedies of Euripides; noted, apparently, for informal morals and sophisticated guile.

MENELAOS: King of Sparta; husband of HELEN, *q.v.*; *see also* GENERAL NOTES for p. 79.

MOLOSSOS: A region in Epeiros noted for its large and alarming sheepdogs.

MUSES: Nine goddesses presiding over the arts and sciences; daughters of Zeus and Mnemosynê ('Memory').

NAUSIKAA: A princess of Phaiakia; daughter of Alkinoös, who befriended Odysseus.

NEMESIS: Divine retribution, occasionally represented as a goddess.

NEREUS: A sea god; father, by his sister Doris, of fifty sea-nymph daughters known as the Nereidês.

NIKIAS: Unfortunate commander of the Athenian forces on the Sicilian Expedition, ignominiously put to death by the enemy upon his surrender at Syracuse.

NILUS: River in Egypt.

OLYMPIAN: Pertaining to OLYMPOS, *q.v.*

OLYMPOS: A mountain in Thessaly; the dwelling of the gods.

OREADES: Nymphs of the mountains.

PALAMEDES: One of the Greek commanders at Troy, ruined by the machinations of his personal enemy Odysseus; subject of a lost tragedy by Euripides; *see* GENERAL NOTES for p. 69.

PALLAS: A name for ATHENA, *q.v.*

PAN: The sylvan god.

PAUSON: A miserly painter (ζωγράφος). He 'burns to multiply the rigours of fasting' because fasting costs no money.

PENELOPE: Wife of Odysseus, perennial model of constancy in marriage.

PERSEPHONE: Daughter of DEMETER, *q.v.*, and wife of PLOUTON; *see* GENERAL NOTES for p. 28.

PERSEUS: Son of Zeus and a mortal girl, Danaê, daughter of Akrisios, king of Argos; *cf.* ANDROMEDA.

PHAIDRA: Wife of King Theseus of Athens; driven mad by the malice of Aphroditê, she attempted to seduce her stepson Hippolytos, and, when he rejected her, accused him to her husband of rape, and committed suicide (*cf.* Genesis XXXIX: 7-22); the subject is brilliantly treated in the *Hippolytos* of Euripides.

PHILOKLES: An unsuccessful tragic poet, nephew of Aischylos.

PHOIBOS: A name for APOLLO, *q.v.*

PHRYNICHOS: Tragic poet, *fl. c.* 500 B.C.

PHRYNONDAS: A swindler of such heroic capacity that he became proverbial; no details are known.

PLOUTOS: Ordinarily the god of wealth (Πλοῦτος), but here assimilated to Ploutôn (Πλούτων)—that is to say, Pluto—as god of Hadês, husband of PERSEPHONE, *q.v.* [Σ]

PNYX: The meeting place of the Assembly at Athens.

POSEIDON: God of the sea.

PROTEAS: *see* GENERAL NOTES for p. 81.

PROTEUS: A legendary king of Egypt; *see* GENERAL NOTES for p. 81.

PYTHIAN: An epithet of the gods as associated with the shrine of Apollo at Delphoi.

SEMELE: The mother, by Zeus, of DIONYSOS, *q.v.*

SIMOIS: A river of Troy.

[SKAMANDROS]: A river of Troy; hence, SKAMANDRIAN.

133

SKIRA: The annual Parasol Festival of Deméter and Persephonê (or, as some say, of Athena) near the beginning of July.

STENIA: A one-day festival preparatory to the THESMOPHORIA, *q.v.*

THEOGNIS: A tragic poet, contemporary of A., whose work was so lifeless that he was nicknamed 'Snow' (Χιών); not to be confused with the melancholically gnomic poet who wrote some hundred years earlier.

THEONOE: An Egyptian princess, daughter of PROTEUS, *q.v.*

THESMOPHORIA: Three-day festival of DEMETER and PERSEPHONE, *qq.v.*; *see also* GENERAL NOTES for p. 28.

TYNDAREUS: A king of Sparta, nominally father of HELEN, *q.v.*

XENOKLES: A dramatist, one of the sons of the poet Karkînos; bitterly derided elsewhere by A.

ZEUS: Father of gods and men.